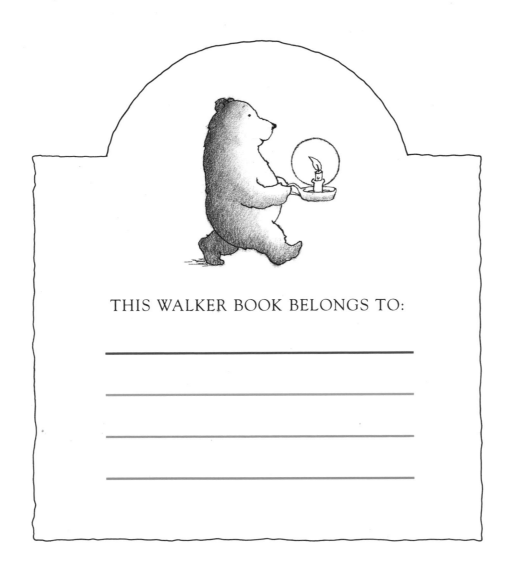

THIS WALKER BOOK BELONGS TO:

_____

_____

_____

_____

For the new gang –
Micha, Amira, Tristan,
Clarke, Matthew and Monica ~ J.H.

For Max ~ **B.G.**

Eyes, Nose,

First published 1999 by Walker Books Ltd
87 Vauxhall Walk, London SE11 5HJ

This edition published 2000

10 9 8 7 6

Text © 1999 Judy Hindley
Illustrations © 1999 Brita Granström

This book has been typeset in Gararond

Printed in China

British Library Cataloguing in Publication Data
A catalogue record for this book is available

ISBN-13: 978-0-7445-7752-5
ISBN-10: 0-7445-7752-7

www.walkerbooks.co.uk

Fingers and Toes

A FIRST BOOK ABOUT YOU

Judy Hindley

illustrated by
Brita Granström

WALKER BOOKS
AND SUBSIDIARIES
LONDON • BOSTON • SYDNEY

Eyes are to blink. Eyes are to wink.
Eyes are for looking and finding – **You!**
Eyes are to shut when you're asleep.
Eyes are for hiding ...

A nose is to blow.

A nose is to sniff.

A nose has holes
for sniffing with.

Ears are to find at
the sides of your head.
Are you wearing your
ears today?
Hurray!
Ears are to hear
a story with.

A mouth is to yawn ...
Open
wide –
See all the teeth
and the tongue
inside?

A mouth is to laugh –

Ha-ha! Ha-ha!

A tongue is to talk
and to sing – La-la!

La-la,

la-la,

la-la!

Lips are to make
very small
for a kiss.

Lips are to whistle
and blow.

Lips are to stretch
very wide for a smile,
and round
when your mouth
goes –
Ho!
Ho!
Ho!

Feel how it makes
your belly go
when you laugh –
Ha-ha!
Hee-hee!
Ho-
ho!

What about necks?
A neck is to tickle.
What about shoulders?
Those are to wriggle.

A back
is to
stretch
so high
and
tall.

A back is
to curl up
snug
and small.

Arms go up,

Arms go down.

Arms go reaching way out wide. Arms can rock you side to side.

Hands
are to hold
and pat

and
clap!

Hands are to
hide
behind your
back.

Fingers and thumbs
are for counting on,

One,
two, three,
four,
five ...

Let's find some toes
and count up those —
And then
let's wiggle
and
waggle each one!

Legs are for leaping and jumping and dancing.

and skipping and hopping.

Legs are for kicking

Feet are for STOMPING.

And suddenly —

STOppING!

Knees are to bend,
so let's all sit down —

BUMP!

On our bottoms, side by side.

So here we are!
And I'll tell you again —
Kisses are little,

smiles are wide ...

A hug is a bundle with YOU inside.